David Tebbe

Barack Obama and the American Dream as Depicted in Some of His Famous Speeches

David Tebbe

Barack Obama and the American Dream as Depicted in Some of His Famous Speeches

GRIN Verlag

Bibliografische Information der Deutschen Nationalbibliothek: Die Deutsche Bibliothek verzeichnet diese Publikation in der Deutschen Nationalbibliografie; detaillierte bibliografische Daten sind im Internet über http://dnb.d-nb.de/ abrufbar.

1. Auflage 2012
Copyright © 2012 GRIN Verlag
http://www.grin.com/
Druck und Bindung: Books on Demand GmbH, Norderstedt Germany
ISBN 978-3-656-19150-6

Barack Obama

And the

American Dream

As Depicted

In Some of His Famous Speeches

David Tebbe

The picture on the front page shows George Frederic Watts´ painting "Hope". It was painted in 1886 and given to the British nation in 1897. Now it is in London's Tate Museum. [http://www.tate.org.uk/servlet/ViewWork?workid=16034] (Last access: 19/03/2012)

When Reverend Wright (using this picture) preached one Sunday in 1990 about the power of hope Obama says he found himself in tears. Suddenly he understood that his bitterness and despair had paralyzed him and that his momma and daddy had thanked God "in advance for all that they dared to hope for in [him]" (Obama, Dreams, 292-295; 295) Now Obama understood that the "Audacity of Hope" is the substance of the American Dream. (Cf. p.11-13)

Index of contents

1. Introduction

In 2009 Barack Obama became the 44th President of the United States. He fascinated millions of people all over the world and even in Germany people recited his motto "Yes we can". He inspired a nation. Obama and his speeches were so electrifying that a lot of people spoke of a national obsession with Senator Barack Obama.

I wondered how he managed to fill the people with enthusiasm. He was always speaking about the American Dream. So I asked myself: "What is this American Dream; which of its values and ideas are so fascinating that they inspired the nation, and how are they influenced by Obama using them in his speeches? Does Obama just use them for tactical reasons because they are so popular?"

In order to answer these questions it is at first necessary to define the term "American Dream" and to understand the history and meaning of its ideas and values. Then I want to look at Obama's biography, if there are any hints that show his interest in the American Dream and what influence does it have on his interpretation of the American Dream.

For the analysis of his interpretation of the American Dream I have chosen a "selection of Obama's most striking speeches up to April 2009"[1]. These speeches show "how he managed...to inspire many citizens".[2] Because I want to illustrate all of the six fundamental concepts of the "American Dream" I scanned the whole collection for striking phrases exemplifying his use of these ideas. They will show his specific interpretation of the American Dream.

2. The American Dream

2.1 Definition

"American Dream" has become a widespread term to describe a set of American values and beliefs. Jim Cullen describes it as an idea that "shaped American identity from the Pilgrims to the present".[3] It is the central idea of the American history, even though its concept is shifting.[4]

---

[1] Obama 2009, p.vi
[2] Ibid.
[3] Cullen, back cover
[4] Ibid.

The term "American Dream" was first used in the book "Drift and Mastery" the journalist Walter Lippmann published in 1914.[5] He used it to motivate people to find a new dream for the 20th century. He was frustrated at the inaction of the American government and politicians. The historian James Truslow Adams popularized the term in 1931. In his book "The Epic of America" he describes how America came into being and what kind of values are typical for most Americans. And he specifies it as "that dream of a land in which life should be better and richer and fuller for every man, with opportunity for each according to ability or achievement"[6]. But Adams was dreaming of something more than individual wealth. He was interested in a more spiritual and less materialistic and a more communal and less individualistic version of the dream: "At its core, the American Dream represents the state of mind – that is, an enduring optimism given to a people who might be tempted to succumb to the travails of adversity, but who, instead, repeatedly rise from the ashes to continue to build a great nation."[7]

Knowing what the "American Dream" is at its core, we have to think about the values and ideas that are associated with it. Even if the number of ideas that are referred to the American Dream is changing there is a broad consensus that it exists of the following six fundamental concepts.[8]

2.2 History of concepts

2.2.1 The belief in social progress

According to the course of the sun from east to west the Middle Ages believed in a development of mankind that has started in the east and would fulfill in the west. The Puritans who fled from Europe to America wanted to build up "a new heaven upon earth".[9] Especially after 1630 Puritans left for New England.[10] They believed "that the world was a corrupt place, but one that could be reformed".[11] They believed due to the Bible that God has sent them to America where they should start the process of realizing the new kingdom of God.[12]

The governor of New England, John Winthrop puts it in his sermon "Christian Charity" in this way: he, Winthrop, is Moses, the leader of the chosen people Israel who is guiding New

---

[5] Cf. Hanson / White, p. 2f
[6] Hanson / White, p. 3
[7] Hanson / White, p. 3
[8] Cf. Freese, 2011, p.71
[9] Freese, 1994, p. 35
[10] Cf. Wikipedia. Puritan
[11] Cullen, 15
[12] Cf. Prexi, p. 6f.

England the steep way through the desert to the mountain top, to the Promised Land, where they can build the "Citty upon a hill", a metaphor taken from Matthew 5:14, where Jesus says at the same time that the Christians are "the light of the world".[13] . They wanted to form a more perfect community than the nation they had left in old Europe. The way up of the chosen People is a "steady progress toward perfection".[14] The main reason that motivated them to cross the Atlantic Ocean was that they didn't want their children to be corrupted; therefore the idea that their "children might have a better life" as themselves has been an essential element of the American Dream.[15]

2.2.2 The belief in individual success

The hope of the Puritans was to be saved for eternal life. If someone is successful that is a sign for being chosen by God; therefore the Puritans always worked hard, carried themselves with discipline, industriousness and asceticism.[16] They had a "concept of individual´s self – responsibility"[17] but at the same time they wanted to establish with their community a "model of Christian charity"[18]. So in the beginning of the settlement, it was more a spiritual than a materialistic understanding of individual success.[19]

This understanding of success changed during the next generations. To them success meant "worldly success"[20]. Benjamin Franklin (1709-1790) for example was interested in material success.[21] Sayings of his "Poor Richard Almanac" like "anyone can pull himself up by his own bootstrings"[22] show, that this generation was convinced, that no one needs helpful connections or the community for his individual success.

Now the people were no longer as the early Puritans interested to form a spiritual community, the paradise on earth. Now they wanted the materialistic "land of unlimited opportunities".[23]

---

[13] Cf. Müller, p. 39-41; in the Bible "to be the light of the world" means to be role models. This idea paved the way for the concept of Manifest Destiny (cf. Prexi, p. 7).
[14] Müller, p.42
[15] Cf. Cullen, p. 16
[16] Cf. Müller, p. 47f.
[17] Freese, ³1994, p.111
[18] Prexi, p. 6
[19] Müller, p.49f.
[20] Müller, p.54
[21] ibid.
[22] Freese, ³1994, p.110
[23] Müller, p. 57

Everybody can rise "from rags to riches", a message that was popularized in the 19th century by Horatio Alger, Jr.[24] He helped to give the American Dream a "materialistic twist".[25]

2.2.3 The belief in the values and rights of the founding documents and famous reflections on it

The Congress of the 13 American colonies adopted the Declaration of Independence on July 4, 1776. Famous is its preamble: "We hold these truths to be self – evident, that all men are created equal, that they are endowed by their Creator with certain unalienable Rights that among these are Life, Liberty and the pursuit of Happiness."[26] These values and rights became an outstanding part of the American Dream.

The Constitution of the United States was adopted in 1787. Often quoted is the beginning of its preamble: "We the People of the United States, in Order to form a more perfect Union, establish Justice, …".[27] The idea of the early Puritans that the world and every community have to be reformed and a steady progress toward perfection is necessary has now become an element of the Constitution. Its first ten amendments, known as the Bill of Rights, guarantee freedoms of religion, press, speech and assembly etc..[28]

President Lincoln underlines in his famous Gettysburg Address the principles of human equality and the survival of America's democracy: "…that government of the people, by the people, for the people, shall not perish from the Earth"[29]. In 1963 Martin Luther King quoted the famous creed of the preamble of the Declaration of Independence: "…We hold these truths to be self – evident, that all men are created equal,…"[30] and the rights that are promised in it "Life, Liberty and the pursuit of Happiness"[31] and spoke of his hope, his dream, that one day the values of equality, freedom and justice will prevail in America.[32]

2.2.4 The belief in the "melting pot" or similar images

These promises of the freedom documents were the basis for the dreams of the people who were suffering under the rules of their governments. Especially since 1820 people of all

---

[24]Cf. Freese, ³1994, p.110f
[25] Freese, ³1994, p.113
[26] Bauer, p. 7
[27] Wikipedia, United States Constitution
[28] Cf. Bauer, p. 8f.
[29] Bauer, p.14
[30] Freese, 2011, p. 23, l. 122-124;
[31] Freese, 2011, p.22, l.25f;
[32]Cf. ibid., p. 22f

nations, religions, races, languages dreaming the American Dream immigrated to the United States. America became a multicultural society, a "melting pot".

This expression became popular in 1908 by Israel Zangwill's play "The Melting Pot", even if its idea was already formulated in 1782.[33] But because the "melting" did not really happen a lot of other images were suggested expressing the peaceful togetherness without mixing: "salad bowl, "patchwork quilt", "E pluribus Unum"[34] ("Out of many, one"). These images illustrate the idea of the American Dream that the union is more than the sum of its parts.

2.2.5 The belief in ever new frontiers

The advance of American settlement westward had a lot of influence on the American Dream. The pioneers made experiences at the frontier between civilization of settlement and the savagery of wilderness that formed the typical American character. That is the very popular thesis of the historian Frederick Jackson Turner he first published in 1893[35].

The pioneers advancing westward had to adapt to environmental challenges again and again. This was a long process by which citizens with strength, individuality, equal opportunities, economic success were formed. Moving forward every generation became more individualistic, more democratic, more optimistic, more self-confident, more distrustful of authority, more American. Crossing the ocean to look for the Promised Land in America and then going westward to continue the pursuit transformed the Americans into a "nation of wanderers".[36] Typical for them is the belief in "ever new beginnings", "an innovative spirit"[37] and the "scorn of older society"[38]

This process was seen as a motor for change and source of America's power. So when the US Census of 1890 stated that this American frontier was closed, many believed America needed new challenges. "America extended its Manifest Destiny to areas beyond the West"[39]. For President Roosevelt (President: 1901-1909) it was necessary that America must expand overseas.[40] For Kennedy the new challenge was the open frontier of space;[41] for others it was

[33] Cf. Freese, ³1994, p.151-153
[34] Cf. Wikipedia ""E pluribus unum": Until 1956, when "In God We Trust" became the official motto, it was considered to be the motto of the nation. Originally it suggested that out of many colonies or states a single nation emerged. Now it is illustrating that out of many people, races etc. a single nation emerged.
[35] Cf. Wikipedia, Frontier Thesis
[36] Billington, p. 2
[37] Cf. Prexi, p. 12
[38] Bauer, p. 21
[39] Müller, p. 70
[40] Cf. Wikipedia, Frontier Thesis
[41] Cf. Ibid.

the open frontier of science, society and internet.[42] So the belief in ever new frontiers is another part of the American dream. This and the idea of a steady progress toward perfection with a better life for the children[43] shaped in my opinion the belief in "the cult of newness", in "ever new beginnings" and "the glorification of youth".[44]

2.2.5 The belief in American Exceptionalism

The Puritans, as we have already stated, paved the way for the concept of Manifest Destiny with their idea that they were – in following God's call- the "Citty upon the Hill", the "light of the world" and God's chosen people. Because this idea does not conform to a pattern or norm this belief is also called American Exceptionalism.

This idea of being a role model survived and is combined with the idea of America's leadership: The first presidents of the young democracy can say that the United States are "acting for mankind"[45](Jefferson) or are "the guardians of freedom to preserve it for the benefit of the human race"[46](Jackson).

President Lincoln[47] links his intention to give freedom to the slaves to the idea that America is the "Citty upon the Hill". And if America doesn't give freedom to the slaves, the world will lose "the last best hope on Earth". But if America saves to be "the last best hope on Earth", "the world will forever applaud and God must forever bless."

The term "Manifest Destiny" first used in 1845 to claim the North American continent for the United States[48] became, after the continent was conquered, a synonym for the policy of expansion and intervention all over the world.[49] In 1917 President Wilson (1913 -1921) gave the idea of Manifest Destiny a new interpretation: America should make "the world safe for democracy" and "encourage the self – determination of all people", an interpretation that is in accordance with President Obama's understanding of America's leadership.[50]

---

[42] Cf. Cullen, p. 143
[43] See above: 2.2.1
[44] For Freese, 2011, p.71, these ideas are "additional concepts" of the "American Dream".
[45] Quoted in Müller, p. 67
[46] Ibid., p.67f.
[47] Cf. Lincoln, Annual Address to the U.S. Congress, 1 December 1862
[48] Cf. Müller, p. 68
[49] Cf. Prexi, p. 13
[50] Cf. Obama, 2006, p. 334

9

2.3. The concept of the American Dream since September 11th 2001

Most presidents of the United States have used the concept of the American Dream to motivate the nation. But since the events of September 11th fear instead of optimism dominated America[51] and at least since 2008 the economic crisis became visible.[52] The disaster of which Obama spoke in August 2008 was real: a "nation […] at war, the economy […] in turmoil and the American promise […] threatened".[53] America was in despair. Nevertheless the faith in the American Dream was still strong. Americans have not stopped dreaming[54] But its meaning shifted from a more material and individual to a more spiritual and communal version of the dream.[55]. This backed up the optimism of the Americans that they could achieve the American Dream.[56] "The Dreamless Dead´- those who do not believe in the American Dream- was one of Obama´s largest support groups during his campaign"[57] and Obama "won the votes of 71% of those who say that the American Dream does not exist."[58] Obama embodies this Dream more than any other president.

3. Biography of Barack Hussein Obama

3.1 Obama´s curriculum vitae

For Obama the American Dream came true. He reached the highest position in the USA because he could back up the optimism of the Americans, after he had rediscovered the more spiritual version of the dream for his own life. To understand this it is at first necessary to have an overview of his life.

3.1.1 Childhood and Adolescence in Hawaii and Indonesia

Hawaii – United States (1961-1967) (up to the age of 6 years) Obama's mother, An Dunhum, and his father, the Kenyan Barack Obama Sr. met in 1960 at the University of Hawai. On August 4th 1961 Barack Hussein Obama was born in Honolulu, Hawaii. His parents divorced in 1964. His father went back to Kenya. In 1966 Obama's mother married an Indonesian man.

---

[51] Cf. Kimmage, p. 34
[52] Cf. ibid.,p. 35
[53] Obama, 2009, p. 90
[54] Cf. Hanson, Whose Dream?, p. 96
[55] Cf. Hanson/White, p. 10; Hanson, Whose dream?, p. 92; Hanson/White, Conclusion, p. 147
[56] Cf.ibid. 148
[57] Ibid. 145
[58] Zogby, p. 111

Jakarta - Indonesia (1967- 1971) (up to the age of 10 years)
In 1967 the family moved to Jakarta, Indonesia. There he attended a local school.

Hawaii – United States (1971-1979) (up to the age of 18 years)
In 1971 his mother sent Obama back to Hawaii for a good education. There he first lived with his grandparents without his mother. He attended a private school. Back in Hawaii he once met his father in 1971. It was the last time he saw him. Obama Sr. died in an automobile accident in 1982. In 1972 Obama's mother returned to Hawaii.

3.1.2 Years of Study

Los Angeles – United States (1979-1981) (up to the age of 20 years)
He studied for two years at a college of Los Angeles.

New York – United States (1981-1983) (up to the age of 22 years)
He studied for two years Political Sciences and graduated from University.in 1983. For a year he worked in different corporations.

Chicago – Illinois - United States (1983-1988) (up to the age of 27 years)
He worked for three years as a community organizer. In this time he joined the Trinity United Church of Christ. In 1987 he travelled for five weeks in Kenya, searching for his relatives and roots.

Cambridge - Massachusetts– United States (1988-1991) (up to the age of 30 years)
He studied at Harvard Law School. At an internship at a law firm in Chicago he met Michelle Robinson. In 1991 he graduated with a Juris Doctor.

3.1.3 Business and Political Career

- 1991 he was back in Chicago. There he was working for a project to mobilize black voters.
- 1992 he married Michelle Robinson. He was teaching constitutional law at the University of Chicago Law School.
- 1993 he started working as a lawyer
- 1995 Obama published his book "Dreams from my Father". His mother died. Her death saddened him deeply.
- 1996-2002 he ran three times for the Illinois State Senate as a Democrat and won the elections.

- 2000 he lost a Democratic primary run for the U.S. House of Representatives.
- 2004 he delivered the keynote speech in support of John Kerry at the Democratic National Convention in Boston. He received 70% of the vote for his election to the United States Senate.
- 2005 he moved as a senator to Washington.
- 2006 he published his book "The Audacity of Hope: Thoughts on Reclaiming the American Dream".
- February 2007 he announced his candidacy for President of the United States.
- June 3rd 2008 he defeated Hillary Clinton for the presumptive nominee for the Democratic Party.
- November 4th 2008 he defeated the Republican presidential nominee John McCain for the position of U.S. President.
- January 20th 2009 he became the 44th President of the United States.

3.2   Obama´s biography and the American Dream[59]

In his childhood in Indonesia Obama noticed for the first time that there are some people who don't like colored skin. Feeling divided between his black and white worlds, he decided that he belonged to the black world. But now he made the experience that being black meant to be angry, to feel powerless and defeated. He began to take drugs. His mother helped him to stop that. But as a mulatto he still didn't know to which world he belonged. This dilemma was still going on in the first years of his study in Los Angeles and New York. With his black friends in New York he shared a common despair. When he worked as a community organizer in Chicago he felt better because he could help black people.

Obama has grown up a skeptic like his mother. But now in Chicago he felt lonely and was thinking about faith. So he was delighted to find a church where he felt at home.[60] At Trinity United Church of Christ in the late 1980s Obama became a Christian. The pastor of this church was the Reverend Wright, who often had visited Africa. Obama could speak with him about his Afro-American identity.

In 1987 he travelled for five weeks in Kenya, searching for his relatives and roots. And there Sarah Obama, the stepmother of his father told him the whole story of his African father and

---

[59] In this passage I am paraphrasing and summarizing Pagel, p. 6-24; any other origin of thoughts I shall indicate.
[60] Krensky, p. 48

grandfather. His grandfather Onyango didn't know to which world he belonged. He admired the whites and at the same time they despised him and called him "house nigger". He became a drinker and an angry old man. And Obama's father, who had worked for the government in Kenya was so stubborn with the government that he lost his work and became a drinker too, because he never got over his bitterness of what had happened to him.

When Obama heard all these things of his grandfather and father, he began to weep. He understood that he with his bitterness, his despair, his frustration of hope was on the same way as his father and grandfather. Obama wrote: "The pain I felt was my father's pain".[61] Obama realized that his father and grandfather in their bitterness and despair couldn't fulfill their dreams.

Then, when Reverend Wright preached one Sunday in 1990 about the power of hope Obama says he found himself in tears. The message of this sermon was: The world is full of pain, despair, hate, apartheid, greed, war, poverty… but in spite of all this the Bible encourages us to the audacity to hope. Such thoughts gave him the encouragement and the belief in "ideas bigger than himself".[62]

Now he didn't feel any longer the despair, the anger and weakness he had felt. His relatives had coined him with the values of freedom, equality and faith in the American Dream. He had understood what the most essential value was: the audacity of hope and why the American Dream didn't fulfill so often for the blacks. They were angry and hate filled against the whites and didn't have the audacity of hope. Obama wrote his memoir "Dreams from my Father" in 1995.

Then he started his political career. But especially many blacks distrusted him. They said: "He isn't black enough." Obama told them that he knew their bitterness and anger and dared to criticize them. Obama knew first-hand they were trapped in their own self-destructive behavior. They had to set aside their roles as victims. With the "audacity of hope" they would have the chance to achieve the American Dream. With the slogan of the American Dream "Pull yourself up by your own bootstraps!" he tried to motivate them.

Many of the black leaders, like Jesse Jackson and even Reverend Wright didn't understand Obama. Jackson said Obama was like a white telling niggers how to behave. But Obama only wanted to help them, because he knew their situation. Their situation had been his own, until

---

[61] Obama, 1995, p. 430
[62] Thomas, p. 112

he discovered the "audacity of hope". Obama realized that not only black people but also a lot of white people of America felt the same despair, anger and hopelessness. Therefore he decided to give people back their belief in justice, equality of chances, their belief in the American Dream.

In 2004 he delivered the keynote speech in support of John Kerry at the Democratic National Convention in Boston. "Barack Obama gave the best speech of his life."[63] He spoke about the values that made America great and of hope in the face of difficulty, the audacity of hope. "In those few minutes, Barack Obama went from being a state politician... to a major figure on the national stage."[64]

Obama never forgot this lesson. The American Dream could inspire people. 2006 he published his book "The Audacity of Hope- Thoughts on Reclaiming the American Dream". In this book he says: "That was the best of the American spirit, I thought – having the audacity to believe despite all the evidence to the contrary that we could restore a sense of community to a nation torn by conflict; the gall to belief that despite personal setbacks.... we had some control – and therefore responsibility – over our own fate. It was that audacity, I thought, that joined us as one people. It was that pervasive spirit of hope that tied my own family's story to the larger American story, and my own story to those of the voters I sought to represent."[65] Obama inspired the nation with the ideas of the American Dream. January 20th 2009 he became the 44th President of the United States.

4. The American Dream in famous speeches of Obama

4.1. Obama´s belief in social progress

Obama shares the idea of the Puritans that the world is a corrupt place but can be reformed in a steady progress towards perfection. This belief is reflected in the preamble of the Constitution of the United States: "We the people of the United States, in Order to form a more perfect union…". Therefore Obama's presidential campaign used the slogans "Change we can believe in" and "Yes We Can". Obama is convinced that the ability to change is the "true genius of America".[66]

---

[63] Krensky, p. 82
[64] Ibid. p. 83f.
[65] Obama, 2006, p. 421
[66] Obama, 2009, p. 127

During his presidential campaign (2008) his pastor Reverend Wright made controversial comments. He damned the United States for its racism and for several other reasons. When Obama was criticized for his pastor he gave a clever statement in response to Wright's controversial remarks. This statement was his speech: "A more perfect Union – "The Race Speech". He opens his speech with the first part of the preamble of the Constitution: "We the people, in order to form a more perfect union."[67].

The core of his clever statement is the fact that he doesn't criticize that Wright has spoken about racism but that he has spoken about the American Society, "as if no progress has been made".[68]

Racism is for Obama "a part of our union that we have not yet made perfect".[69] But "society can change".[70] Both the Declaration of Independence and the Constitution know that Americans are not perfect but they, like the nation itself, implicate the "capacity to be made perfect". [71] The society must "continue on the path of a more perfect union".[72] The metaphor "path" associates these words with the idea of the early Puritans and then of Martin Luther King that the chosen people is on its way to the "Citty upon a hill" or on its way to the mountain top.

Even if the "union may never be perfect"[73], there is a steady improvement of individual, communal and social conditions of existence. The past has shown that the "union can always be perfected"[74], a lesson Obama was already taught by his mother.[75] The achieved improvements give the "audacity of hope" for a better future.[76]

The hope of "a band of colonists" made the United States independent.[77] As they believed in social progress and hoped that their "children might have a better life as themselves" so do the

[67] Obama, 2009, p. 41
[68] Obama, 2009, p. 55
[69] Obama, 2009, p. 49
[70] Obama, 2009, p. 55
[71] Obama, 2009, p. 131
[72] Obama, 2009, p. 54
[73] Obama, 2009, p. 59
[74] Ibid.
[75] Cf. Obama, 2009, p. 4
[76] Cf. Obama, 2009, p. 55f.; Obama uses this expression of Reverend Wright in this context to demonstrate, that to his opinion Wright doesn't follow his own sermon "The audacity to hope".
[77] Cf. Obama, 2009, p. 28

Americans today; they are dreaming of a better future for the children and grandchildren[78] and they want to see their "children climb higher" than they did.[79]

4.2   Obama´s belief in individual success

In the history of the American Dream the belief in individual success changed, as we have seen, from a more spiritual understanding of the early Puritans who aspired a perfect community to a more materialistic understanding of individual success of the following more secularized generations, who were more egoistic and self-serving.

Now it is interesting that Obama underlines the belief in individual success as he, like the Puritans, states that everybody is responsible for himself, but he corrects the undesirable selfish trend that has more and more dominated the American Society and politics up to him with arguments that could have been arguments of the early Puritans - the Bible and the more perfect community: "That's the promise of America - the idea that we are responsible for ourselves, but that we also rise or fall as one nation; the fundamental belief that I am my brother's keeper; I am my sister´s keeper."[80]

As the Puritans, he knows, that a more perfect community requires "a new spirit of service"[81], courage and hard work. He motivates his people and calls America "the hardest-working people on Earth"[82] and praises the "enduring spirit of an America that does not quit".[83] But that is not enough. He launched his campaign for the presidency because he noticed "that the most fundamental American ideal, that a better life is in store for all those willing to work for it was slipping out of reach"[84] And it was slipping out of reach because there were divides between the values of self-reliance, individual liberty on one side and national unity on the other side;[85] between "the promise that says government cannot solve all our problems" on one side and the necessity that it should do "what we cannot do for ourselves".[86] Obama wants "to heal these divides that have held back the progress".[87]. He wants "to reclaim the American Dream and to reaffirm that fundamental truth – that out of many we are one".[88]

---

[78] Cf. Obama, 2009, p. 42
[79] Cf. Obama, 2009, p. 134
[80] Obama, 2009, p. 97; cf. p. 56
[81] Obama, 2009, p. 125
[82] Obama, 2009, p. 153
[83] Obama, 2009, p. 185
[84] Obama, 2009, p. 132
[85] Obama, 2009, p. 125-126
[86] Obama, 2009, p. 96f.
[87] Obama, 2009, p. 126
[88] Obama, 2009, p. 129

Therefore America needs a new declaration of independence, an "independence from selfishness – an appeal not to our easy instincts but to our better angels".[89] The "recognition of the common good" doesn't negate but serves the "individual liberty".[90] "Individual responsibility and mutual responsibility – that's the essence of America's promise".[91]

So it seems as if Obama combines the early Puritan's "concept of individual's self - responsibility" with their interest in a "model of Christian charity". But he's also speaking to non-Christians. Therefore he is stressing the "common good"[92] and not "charity". But however, he wants to correct the selfish materialistic twist of the original belief in individual success and tries to reclaim the American Dream.

4.3   Obama's belief in values and rights of the founding documents and famous reflections on it

Central ideas of the American Dream are values and rights like equality, democracy, life, liberty, the pursuit of happiness and personal freedoms which are stated and promised in the founding documents of the United States. Many people think that these values and rights of the founding documents are the foundation for all American Dreams. But a lot of Americans had stopped dreaming. Therefore Obama tries to reclaim the American Dream and is talking in his election campaign about his father and mother who "shared a belief that in America, their son could achieve whatever he put his mind to".[93] The reason for it is the promise given in the Declaration of Independence and the courage that keeps it alive so that everybody can pursue his individual dreams if he works hard enough.[94]

Obama wants to encourage the nation: change happens; and as the dream of Martin Luther King who dreamed of equality comes true step-by-step, so the promise of America will fulfill again if America walks together and holds firmly to the hope it confesses.[95]

Obama, as shown above, criticizes Reverend Wright in the "Race speech" because he has spoken about the American society as if no progress has been made. His argument: both the

---

[89] Obama, 2009, p. 132
[90] Obama, 2009, p. 153
[91] Obama, 2009, p. 101
[92] Obama, 2009, p. 142
[93] Obama, 2009, p. 90
[94] Ibid.
[95] Cf. Obama, 2009, p. 107-109

Declaration of Independence and the Constitution implicate the capacity respectively the values to make the Union more and more perfect.[96]

Most of the immigrants were dreaming of those values and rights of the founding documents. Obama's father was fond of discussing this promise of the American Dream. When he was living in Hawaii and someone called him "nigger", he gave a lecture on the "promise of the American dream, and the universal rights of man".[97] He had left Kenya because he was dreaming of the "freedom and opportunity promised by the West"[98].

But the experiences of despair of his father, grandfather and of himself motivated Obama to encourage people to believe that they have the chance to fulfill their dreams. Therefore he starts the Election Night Victory Speech with the reference to "the dream of [America's] founders" and the conclusion that the "power of America's democracy" is still alive.[99] He wants to demonstrate that his story is their story. Therefore he says: "This is your victory" and quotes Lincoln's Gettysburg Address. Their victory has proved that the "government of the people, by the people and for the people has not perished from this Earth."[100] The young people could get rid of their "apathy"[101]. They didn't despair and voted for change. He had succeeded in inspiring his nation with the ideas of the American Dream and here especially with values of the founding documents and Lincoln's and King's reflections on it.

Now it is surprising that he uses this principle and similar values of the American Dream even if speaking to Europeans. Being president Obama is interested in perfecting the international cooperation in "The European Speech". After speaking about all the common challenges[102] he sums it up with the words "change is possible"…"because of three reasons". These reasons are the common values like "life, liberty and the pursuit of happiness" (he puts them on a level with liberte´, egalité, fraternité) the "persistence in the face of difficulty" and the belief in the "new generation"[103]. This shows that Obama uses the ideas of the American Dream, the belief in values, (and in ever new frontiers and in social progress) not only in America but every time when he wants to encourage people to overcome challenges.

---

[96] Cf. Obama, 2009, p. 41
[97] Cf. Obama, 1995, p. 11
[98] Cf. Obama, 2009, p. 75
[99] Cf. Obama, 2009, p. 121
[100] Cf. Obama, 2009, p. 124
[101] Cf. ibid.
[102] Cf. Obama, 2009, p. 188-199
[103] Cf. Obama, 2009, p. 199f.

4.4   Obama´s belief in the ideas of multicultural mixture

The belief in the idea of the "melting pot" or more recent concepts and images illustrate the idea of the American Dream that very different immigrants can be fused into one new nation or better: that the union is more than the sum of its parts.

Obama underlines that America "beneath all the differences of race and region, faith and station" is "one people"[104]. And he points out the peaceful togetherness without mixing speaking of the "patchwork heritage" of the Americans: "For we know that our patchwork heritage is a strength, not a weakness. We are a nation of Christians and Muslims, Jews and Hindus – and non-believers. We are shaped by every language and culture, drawn from every end of this Earth"[105].

In his speech "A More Perfect Union" he responds to controversial remarks of his pastor Reverend Wright, who damned the United States for its racism and for several other reasons. Wright´s remarks involved the risk to divide the races and the nation. In this situation Obama uses the illustration "E Pluribus Unum" and points out "the idea that this nation is more than the sum of its parts – that out of many, we are truly one."[106]

Obama has the same interest to emphasize the Union when he just had been elected President of the United States. In his Victory Speech he not only tries to reconcile the Republicans and the Democrats.[107] He wants "to heal the divides that have held back [the] progress"[108]. Therefore he says: "… in this country, we rise or fall as one nation, as one people".[109] And above all, he wants America to stand together for the change and the progress that is necessary "to reclaim the American Dream and reaffirm that fundamental truth – that out of many, we are one"[110].

To sum it up: Obama uses these illustrations of the American Dream to express the multicultural heritage and to back up and assist the peaceful togetherness of the American nation.

---

[104] Cf. Obama, 2009, p. 19
[105] Obama, 2009, p. 143
[106] Cf. Obama, 2009, p. 43
[107] Cf. Obama, 2009, p. 121
[108] Cf. Obama, 2009, p. 126
[109] Cf. Obama, 2009, p. 125f
[110] Cf. Obama, 2009, p. 129

19

4.5   Obama´s belief in ever new frontiers

The westward movement from Europe to America and from the East of America to the West converted the Americans into a "nation of wanderers". They had to cross oceans, had to find "a way out of no way",[111] had to climb mountains, push boundaries, overcome obstacles and challenges. Therefore it is typical that Americans associate the idea of ever new frontiers if they hear expressions of semantic fields like "way", frontier, "obstacle", "challenge" in the context of this American history.

President Obama's Inaugural Address is a speech that deals with the challenges America has to overcome. After he has named the challenges[112] and said that they are real, serious and many, he starts to encourage his people in reaffirming America's enduring spirit and the promise of the preamble of the Declaration of Independence (equality, liberty, pursuit of happiness). He does this in reminding them of America's "better history".[113]

America's "journey has never been one of shortcuts or settling for less. It has not been the path for the fainthearted..... Rather, it has been the risk-takers, the doers, the makers of things...who have carried us up the long, rugged path towards prosperity and freedom"[114]. He speaks of their travelling across oceans, settling the West, fighting, struggling, sacrificing, working, and concludes: "This is the journey we continue today."[115]

What Obama describes here is the "enduring spirit"[116] of a "nation of wanderers" with traits of the frontier like energy, strength, inventive skills, buoyancy, toughness, industriousness[117]. And with a view to the challenges America has to face now and with the view to their grandchildren, he tries to motivate them not "to let this journey end."[118] This journey is the "path of a more perfect union".[119] Obama knows "that there are roadblocks that stand in our path".[120] But "there is no obstacle [they] can't overcome".[121]

In his "Election Night Victory Speech" Obama wants to be realistic but at the same time he wants to motivate his people: "The road ahead will be long. Our climb will be steep...but

---

[111] Obama, 2009, p. 51
[112] Cf. Obama, 2009, p. 137f
[113] Obama, 2009, p. 138
[114] Obama, 2009, p. 139
[115] Cf. Obama, 2009, p. 139f
[116] Obama, 2009, p. 138
[117] Billington, p. 2-8; Turner, p. 9-14.
[118] Cf. Obama, 2009, p. 147
[119] Cf. Obama, 2009, p. 54
[120] Cf. Obama, 2009, p. 27
[121] Cf. Obama, 2009, p. 112

20

America… we as a people will get there."[122] And in his "Speech at Lincoln's 200th Birthday" he again speaks of earlier American generations and says: "… it is precisely when we are in the deepest valley, when they climb is steepest, that Americans relearn how to take the mountaintop."[123] The reason for it is "that American spirit – that American promise – that pushes us forward even when the path is uncertain;…That makes us fix our eye… on… that better place around the bend. …that has led immigrants to cross oceans and pioneers to travel West."[124]

These quotations convey that not only the semantic fields like " way", frontier, "obstacle", "challenge" indicate that Obama uses ideas of the American dream to inspire the Americans. Sometimes he refers directly to the westward movement of the pioneers.

The last quotation shows, that for Obama the experience of the frontier doesn't start with the pioneers going westwards. It started already earlier with the immigrants crossing the ocean westwards. And it didn't stop when the American frontier in 1890 was declared closed. There are always new frontiers, new challenges-in politics, society and science.

Therefore you can read in "Obama's Letter to His Daughters": "I want us to push the boundaries of discovery so that you'll live to see new technologies and inventions that improve our lives and make our planet cleaner and safer. And I want us to push our own human boundaries to reach beyond the divides of race and region, gender and religion that keep us from seeing the best in each other."[125]

The belief that ever new frontiers, new boundaries of land, politics, society and science are to be crossed and obstacles to be surmounted that is an idea of the American dream that can be found in Obama´s speeches. He uses it to motive a nation, especially the "Dreamless Dead" to find the way out of no way, to overcome obstacles and not to let the journey of a more perfect union end.

4.6 Obama´s belief in American Exceptionalism

The Puritans believed as we have demonstrated above, that they were following God´s call and that they were the "Citty upon the Hill", the "light of the world" and "God´s chosen people". This idea of being a role model survived and was combined with the idea of

---

[122] Cf. Obama, 2009, p. 125
[123] Cf. Obama, 2009, p. 156
[124] Cf. Obama, 2009, p. 108
[125] Obama, 2009, p. 4

21

America's leadership. President Lincoln coined for all these ideas the phrase that America is "the last best hope on Earth". The 19th century called this belief in American Exceptionalism: "Manifest Destiny" This term was used to justify the policy of expansion on the North American continent and then America´s expansion and intervention all over the world. The 20th century reinterpreted the idea that way that America should export the idea of democracy and its other ideals to other countries and should encourage the self-determination of all people.

With the exception that Obama doesn't justify America's expansion all over the world, you can find all the above named elements of the belief in American Exceptionalism in Obama's speeches. He can say that "the knowledge that God calls on us to shape an uncertain destiny" is the promise and confidence of America.[126] I think even if Obama doesn't mention God expressly he is speaking of God's call, when he says that "destiny [is] calling"[127] or that America is "called to do great things".[128] Obama uses this element that God calls, to make clear, that people have to take responsibility and become active for the duties to themselves, the nation and the world,[129] for the perfection of their union[130] and for the challenges America has to face.[131]

It is interesting that Obama can broaden this idea if speaking to a different country. "The Berlin Speech" is an example for it. There he is speaking about the war in Afghanistan, the spread of the "deadly Atom", the global warming etc. And at the end of the speech he sums it up: "People of Berlin – and people of the world – the scale of our challenge is great. ... We are people of improbable hope. With an eye to toward the future... let us... answer our destiny, and remake the world once again."[132] So God or destiny calls Berlin and the world. If Obama wants to motivate people to become active and to take responsibility he can broaden the idea that destiny calls the world.

But in spite of this Obama doesn't doubt that America's is the "light the world"[133] and that "America's beacon still burns ... bright".[134] It reminds me of the idea of the "Citty upon the Hill", when Obama in his "First Address to Joint Session of US Congress" says: "as we stand

---

[126] Cf. Obama, 2009, p. 146
[127] Obama, 2009, p. 20
[128] Cf. Obama, 2009, p. 156
[129] Cf. Obama, 2009, p. 145
[130] Cf. Obama, 2009, p. 20
[131] Cf. Obama, 2009, p. 156
[132] Obama, 2009, p. 87
[133] Cf. Obama, 2009, p. 131; 142
[134] Obama, 2009, p. 127

at this crossroads of history, the eyes of all people in all nations are once again upon us – watching to see what we do with this moment; waiting for us to lead.[135]

In this quotation you can find already the next element of the belief in American Exceptionalism - the belief in America's leadership. Speaking about the foreign policy problems of the Bush era, Obama postulates: "We must once again have the courage and conviction to lead the free world."[136] Being elected president Obama is confident again and states in his Victory Speech: "… a new dawn of American leadership is at hand"[137]; and in his Inaugural Address to his audience in the world, "to all the other peoples and governments who are watching today": America is "ready to lead once more"[138] and "must play its role in ushering in a new era of peace".[139] America has "duties to… the world."[140]

When Obama in the context of America's leadership is speaking of America's ideals like democracy, liberty, opportunity and hope, this shows that he has a sense of mission.[141] But it is abundantly clear when he says that the victory against America's enemies "will only come by…. exporting those ideals that bring hope and opportunity to millions of people around the globe.[142]

It is interesting that Obama, speaking to Europeans, who he thinks might "blame America for much of what's bad" can speak of "Europe's leading role in the word",[143] if he wants to motivate them to take responsibility, become active and "bear their share of the burden" to "forge common solutions to …common problems".[144]

Obama also knows that America's leadership depends on its "moral standing"[145] and on its image to be the "last, best hope on Earth".[146]

All in all it is quite obvious that Obama shares the belief in American Exceptionalism. He makes use of it to encourage people to take responsibility and become active. But he also uses elements of this idea to encourage Non-Americans and says that American Exceptionalism

---

[135] Obama, 2009, p. 182
[136] Obama, 2009, p. 68
[137] Obama, 2009, p. 126
[138] Obama, 2009, p. 137
[139] Obama, 2009, p. 143
[140] Cf. Obama, 2009, p. 145
[141] Cf. Obama, 2009, p. 126
[142] Obama, 2009, p. 17
[143] Cf. Obama, 2009, p. 192
[144] Cf. Obama, 2009, p. 193
[145] Cf. Obama, 2009, p. 103
[146] Cf. Obama, 2009, p. 73; 103; 157

depends on America's moral standing. That shows that he understands this idea in a more spiritual way.

That goes with his attitude that he excludes the policy of brutal expansion. Obama condemns it because it damages the "moral standing" of America: "Of course, manifest destiny also meant bloody and violent conquest.... that... contradicted America's founding principles ..., a conquest that American mythology has always had difficulty fully absorbing but that other countries recognized for what it was – an exercise in raw power."[147]

5. Results

The term "American Dream" is an idea that shaped America's identity from the Pilgrims up to the present. The term itself was first used in the beginning of the 20th century and meant at its core the "enduring optimism" given to the American nation that was tempted to succumb to the travails of adversity. This term summed up and described the strong belief in several ideas, which were shaped in the history of the United States. The concept of the American Dream shifted.

In the beginning of the 21th century the Americans believed in a more individualistic and materialist version of the Dream. Obama rediscovered the more spiritual version of the dream in his life and tried to reclaim it for the nation. Therefore he very often refers to it in his famous speeches and complies with the understanding of the "American Dream" of Lippmann and Adams, who first coined the term.

He shares the belief in social progress. Therefore he doesn't have to look back in bitterness like others. He is free to save all his energy for a better future. And he tries to inspire the nation to do the same; to continue on the path of a more perfect union.

He shares the belief in individual success. But he tries to correct the selfish materialistic trend that is more and more dominating the American society and twisting the original idea, so that success, for those who are willing to work for it, is slipping out of reach. And he does it with arguments that could have been arguments of the early Puritans: the Bible, the more perfect community and the common good.

---

[147] Obama, 2006, p. 332

24

He shares the belief that the values and rights of the founding documents are the substance of the American Dream. But he is using similar values and rights if he wants to inspire Europeans to perfect international cooperation and if he wants to encourage them to overcome common challenges.

Obama shares the belief that the union is more than the sum of its parts and he uses the images of multicultural mixture to back up the peaceful togetherness of the American nation.

He shares the belief in the "enduring spirit" of a "nation of wanderers". He uses this idea to inspire the Americans "not to let the journey end", because this journey is the "path of a more perfect union". They shall believe that they can overcome obstacles and that there is a "better place around the bend", a "better history".

And at last: Obama shares the belief in the American Exceptionalism. But he condemns the policy of brutal expansion because it damages the "moral standing" of America. Instead of that he makes use of it to encourage people, even Europeans, to take responsibility and become active.

6. Conclusion

Obama knows first-hand the despair of feeling angry, powerless and defeated. In the 21st century that has become more and more the situation of America. Therefore he wants to inspire the nation, to restore its audacity of hope, to encourage the nation to take responsibility and become active again, to form a more perfect country and reclaim the American Dream. A dream that, as John Truslow Adam has described it, "at its core... represents a state of mind – that is, an enduring optimism given to a people who might be tempted to succumb to the travails of adversity, but who, instead, repeatedly rise from the ashes to continue to build a great nation". Seeing that people and nations all over the world might be "tempted to succumb to the travails of adversity" this dream is for Obama not only the American Dream but the dream of mankind.

In the beginning I asked myself: Does Obama just use the values and ideas of the American Dream for tactical reasons because they are so popular or does he have a special biographical interest in it; and if so, what is it? Now we know the biographical interest. But does this exclude that he uses the American Dream also for tactical reasons to become president of the United States?

25

Obama knows at least "what one voice can do. That one voice can change a room. And if a voice can change a room, it can change a city,... state,... nation,... world."[148] But does it mean that he will abuse his influence? You never know. But I don´t think so; and it is good to know that one of the mightiest men in the world believes in the audacity of hope.

---

[148] Obama, 2009, p. 119

26

7. Index of Literature

Bauer, Hannspeter: The American Dream, Inventing a Nation, in: Thaler, Engelbert (ed.): Topics for Advanced Learners, Braunschweig, Paderborn, Darmstadt, Schöningh, 2009

Billington, Ray Allen (ed.): Introduction, in: The Frontier Thesis, Valid Interpretation of American History?, p. 1-8 , Malabar, Florida, Krieger Publishing Company, 1977 (original edition 1966)

Cullen, Jim: The American Dream, A Short History of an Idea That Shaped a Nation, New York, 2004 (first published New York, 1962)

Frank, Harald: Rhetorische Analyse der "Yes we can" Rede von Barack Obama, New Hampshire Primary Speech am 08 Januar 2008, Norderstedt, 2008

Freese, Peter: "America", Dream or Nightmare?, Reflections on the Composite Image, Essen, ³1994

Freese, Peter (ed.): Viewfinder Topics, New Edition plus, The American Dream, Humankind's Second Chance?, Berlin and Munich, Langenscheidt KG, 2011

Hanson, Sandra L., White, John Kenneth: The American Dream in the 21st Century, Philadelphia, Pennsylvania, 2011

Hanson, Sandra L.: **Whose Dream?** Gender and the American Dream, in: White, John Kenneth / Hanson, Sandra L (ed.): The American Dream in the 21st Century , Temple University Press, Philadelphia, Pennsylvania, 2011, p.77-103

Hanson, Sandra L./ **White,** John Kenneth: The Making and Persistence of the American Dream, in: White, John Kenneth / Hanson, Sandra L (ed.): The American Dream in the 21st Century , Temple University Press, Philadelphia, Pennsylvania, 2011, p.1-26

Hanson, Sandra L./ **White,** John Kenneth: **Conclusion**: The American Dream: Where Are We?, in: White, John Kenneth / Hanson, Sandra L (ed.): The American Dream in the 21st Century , Temple University Press, Philadelphia, Pennsylvania, 2011, p.141-148

Kimmage, Michael C.: The politics of the American dream, 1982 to 2008, in: White, John Kenneth / Hanson, Sandra L (ed.): The American Dream in the 21st Century , Temple University Press, Philadelphia, Pennsylvania, 2011, p.27-39

Krensky, Stephen: Barack Obama, Biography, New York, DK Publishing, 2010

27

Lincoln, Abraham: Annual Address to the U.S. Congress, 1 December 1862):
http://showcase.netins.net/web/creative/lincoln/speeches/congress.htm (Last access: 19.03.2012)

Müller, Peter: Star Trek, The American Dream Continued? - The Crisis of the American Dream in the 1960s and its Reflection in a contemporary TV Series, Magisterarbeit Studiengang Anglistik/Geschichte, Oldenburg 1994; Stand 04/2003

Obama, Barack: Dreams from My Father, A Story of Race and Inheritance, New York, Random House, Inc., Copyright **1995,** 1st pbk. Ed. 2004

Obama, Barack, The Audacity of Hope, Thoughts on Reclaiming the American Dream, New York, Random House, Inc., **2006,** 1st Vintage Books Ed. 2008

Obama, Barack: Inspire a Nation, Sammlung seiner besten Reden, Vom Wahlkampf bis zur Präsidentschaft 2009, German/English - bilingual edition, ed. by Roaul Heinze with Christian Meyer, Leipzig, Amazon Distribution GmbH, **2009**

Pagel, Carla, Barack Obama – the first African-American US – President, The American Dream, Norderstedt, GRIN Verlag, 2011

Prexi, Lydia, Der Amerikanische Traum: Hintergrund und Kernelemente, Studienarbeit, Norderstedt, GRIN Verlag, 2009

Schmidt – Nagel, Bernd C., Barack Obama and the American Dream, Analysis of different speeches with special focus on the American Dream, Norderstedt, GRIN Verlag, 2011

Schnell, Hildegard, The American Dream, Norderstedt, GRIN Verlag, 2006

Thomas, Garen, Yes we can, A Biography of President Barack Obama, Harrisonburg, Virginia, Donnelley & Sons Company, 2011 (first published 2008)

Turner, Frederick J.: Statement of the Frontier Thesis, in Billington, Ray Allen (ed.): The Frontier Thesis, Valid Interpretation of American History?, p. 9-20 , Malabar, Florida, Krieger Publishing Company, 1977 (original edition 1966)

Wikipedia, E pluribus unum: http://en.wikipedia.org/wiki/E_pluribus_unum (Last access: 19/03/2012)

Wikipedia, Frontier Thesis: http://en.wikipedia.org/wiki/Frontier_Thesis (Last access: 19/03/2012)

Wikipedia, Puritan: http://en.wikipedia.org/wiki/Puritan (Last access: 19/03/2012)

Wikipedia, United States Constitution: http://en.wikipedia.org/wiki/United_States_Constitution (Last access: 19/03/2012)

28

Zogby, John: Want Meets Necessity in the New American Dream, in: White, John Kenneth / Hanson, Sandra L (ed.): The American Dream in the 21st Century , Temple University Press, Philadelphia, Pennsylvania, 2011, p.105-116